COMPLEAT
TANGLER

By Norman Thelwell

Three Sheets in the Wind
Up the Garden Path
Compleat Tangler
Play it as it Lies

.thelwell.
COMPLEAT
TANGLER

Allison & Busby Limited
11 Wardour Mews
London W1F 8AN
allisonandbusby.com

First published in 1967.
This paperback edition published by Allison & Busby in 2023.

A CIP catalogue record for this book is available from
the British Library.

10 9 8 7 6 5 4 3 2 1

ISBN 978-0-7490-2917-3

Typeset in 10/15 pt Adobe Caslon Pro by
Allison & Busby Ltd.

The paper used for this Allison & Busby publication
has been produced from trees that have been legally sourced
from well-managed and credibly certified forests.

Printed and bound by
CPI Group (UK) Ltd, Croydon, CR0 4YY

CONTENTS

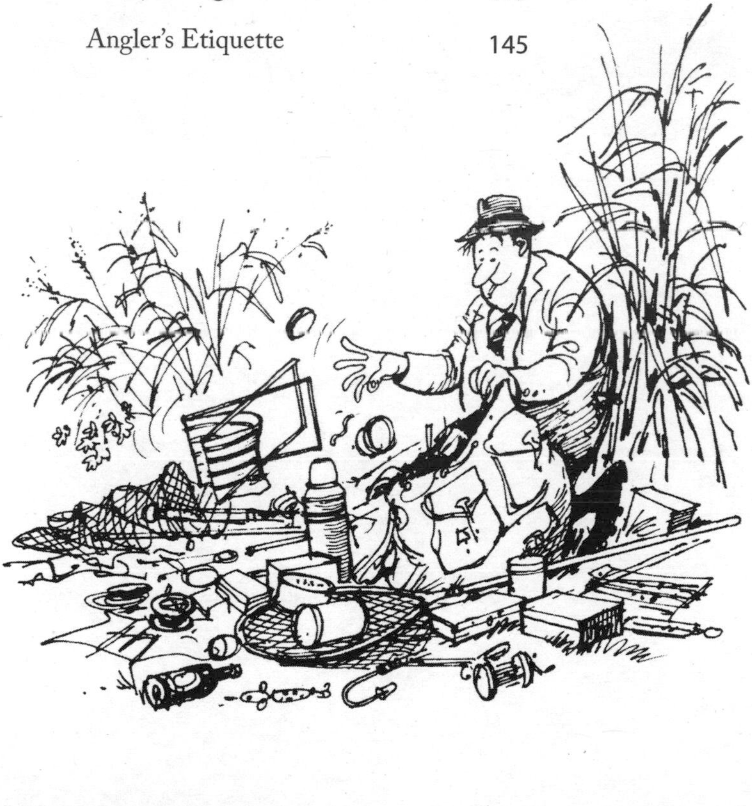

TECHNICAL TERMS
EXPLAINED

A slipping clutch

Hook to gut

A bloody butcher

River report

Bleak

Trotting the water

15

Swan shot

A salmon lie

No. 2 hook

Fish's window

Lob worm

Blue upright

Pale watery

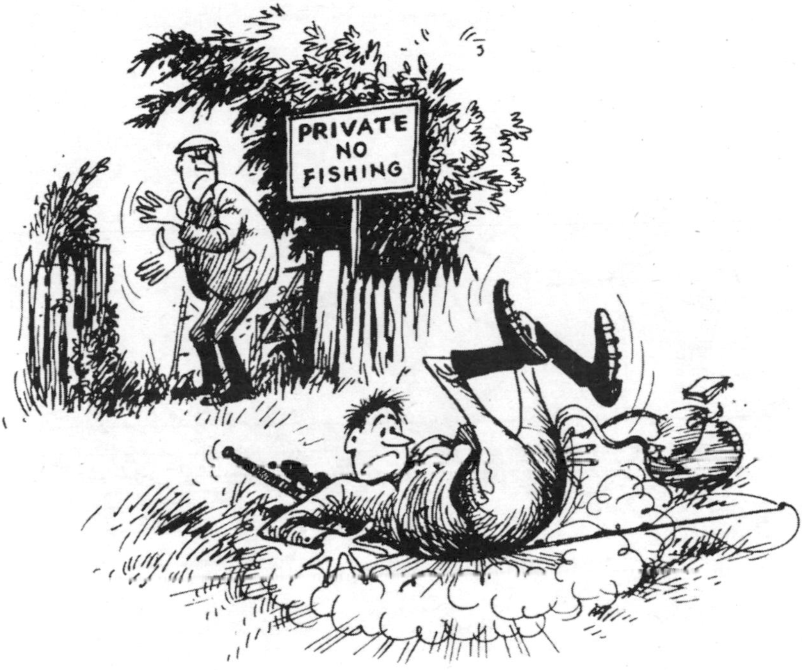
PRIVATE
NO
FISHING

A disgorger

Miller's thumb

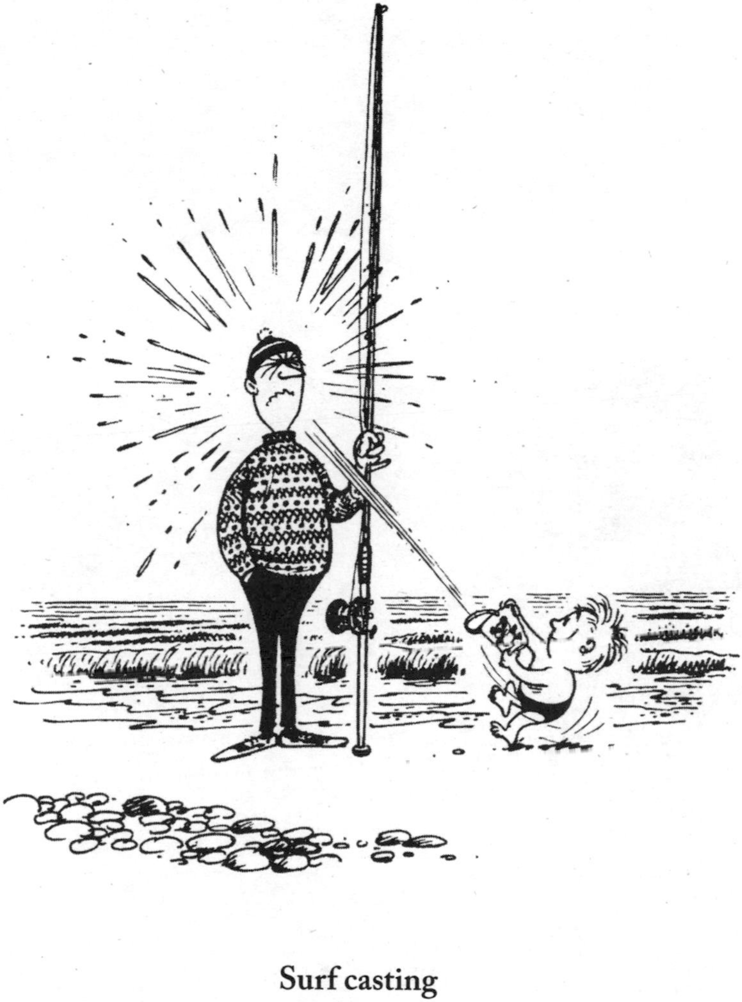

Surf casting

Hairy Mary

Terminal tackle

ANGLER'S GLORY

There are many reasons why men go fishing.

For some it means escape from the noise and
turmoil of everyday life.

For others, it is a change from the monotony of sitting on an office stool all day.

Some regard angling as an exact science.

Others are drawn by its exciting uncertainties.

But for most men it is the love of a fresh wind on the face

and the enchanting sound of running water.

It is the primitive joy of hunting wild creatures . . .

of pitting his own wits against their natural cunning

and overcoming their resistance by sheer skill.

When fish are on the feed – there is nothing quite like
the suppressed excitement of tackling up . . .

of selecting exactly the right bait . . .

of feeling the balance and whip of a favourite rod

and making the first cast.

The experienced angler is prepared for little snags of course
and knows the most scientific way to deal with them.

Half his pleasure lies in manipulating his beloved tackle

and solving technical problems.

But once his tackle is among the fish . . .

he is the happiest of men.

He can savour the strange thrill of being utterly alone . . .

tingle to the sharp excitement of the day's first bite

and know the satisfaction of making a successful strike.

He can lean back in contentment on cowslip banks

and let everything wash over him.

But there are other pleasures still for the fisherman's delight – for nature is everywhere about him.

**For company – he has the friendly, short-sighted
little water vole**

and nature's own anglers to admire.

Who but he knows the haunting boom of the bittern

and the music of the mute swan's wing?

His days are spent among the purple loosestrife
and wild iris . . .

where the air is heavy with the scents of earth and water.

He is familiar with the silent swoop of the evening bat

and the mating dance of the blue-winged olives
in the gloaming.

He knows the rippling shallows

and deep pools.

Unselfish by nature – he delights to show the novice
where the big chub cruise

and where the best pike lie.

And, when he lands a fish, he will rarely kill it – but
will watch it return to the water – happy to see
it free once more . . .

to give sport to some brother angler.

BROTHERS
OF THE ANGLE

Fishermen think of themselves as one big family

and treat each other accordingly.

They have evolved over the years into
three distinct species.

The largest of these is the COARSE FISHERMAN

He is happy to take almost any kind of fish . . .

from any kind of water.

He collects a wide range of tackle and knows precisely
how to use it.

He is a great believer in specially prepared baits.

His ranks have divided into three sub-species:
(1) THE SERIOUS MATCH ANGLER – interested in
nothing but catching fish.

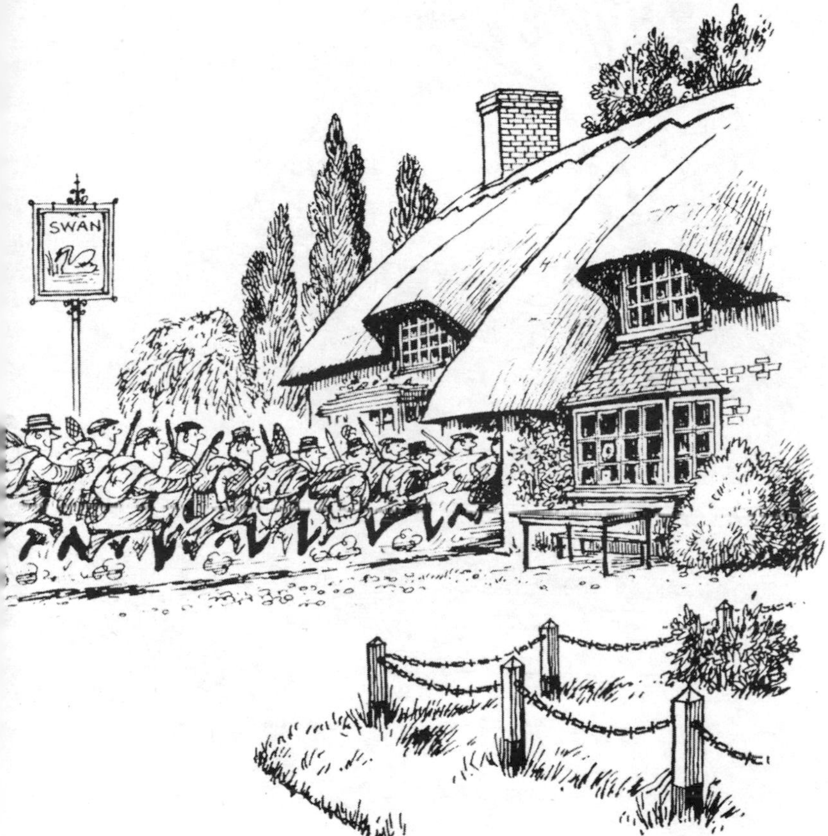
SWAN

(2) THE SOLITARY 'PLEASURE' FISHERMAN – whose
one desire . . .

is to get away from it all.

And (3) THE SPECIMEN HUNTER – content to wait
weeks for his quarry

and contemptuous of anything . . .

which does not break a record.

THE GAME MEN

The most exclusive of all anglers is the
DRY FLY MAN.

He likes to study the river from a Bentley

and is interested only in water as clear as gin – and twice
as expensive.

He puts a lorry load of trout into his water every spring

and employs experts to ensure that they never get out.

He spends many hours studying minute aquatic flies
which his trout very rarely eat

and tying imitations – which look nothing like
the real ones.

Fishing is his sole form of exercise – but he considers
it bad form to move more than his wrist when casting.

He can identify a fly taken by a trout – at fifty yards range and he wears special dark glasses to do it.

But he cannot see an imitation twelve inches away.

He hooks his favourite flies conveniently into his tweed
clothing – where nothing can remove them when needed

. . . except the wind.

THE WET FLY MAN is a more active creature

and spends a good deal of time in the water.

He is less vain about his appearance.

He rarely sees his fish until he has hooked it . . .

unlike **THE SALMON MAN.**

Salmon do not feed in fresh water, so the angler's only hope is to aggravate them. Nevertheless – the salmon exerts a particularly strong hold . . .

. . . on its adherents

and it is frequently taken on both fly and spinner.

THE SEA ANGLERS

These hardy fishermen enjoy one of the most exciting
and invigorating sports in the world.

There is a warm feeling of brotherhood among all those
who love messing about in boats –

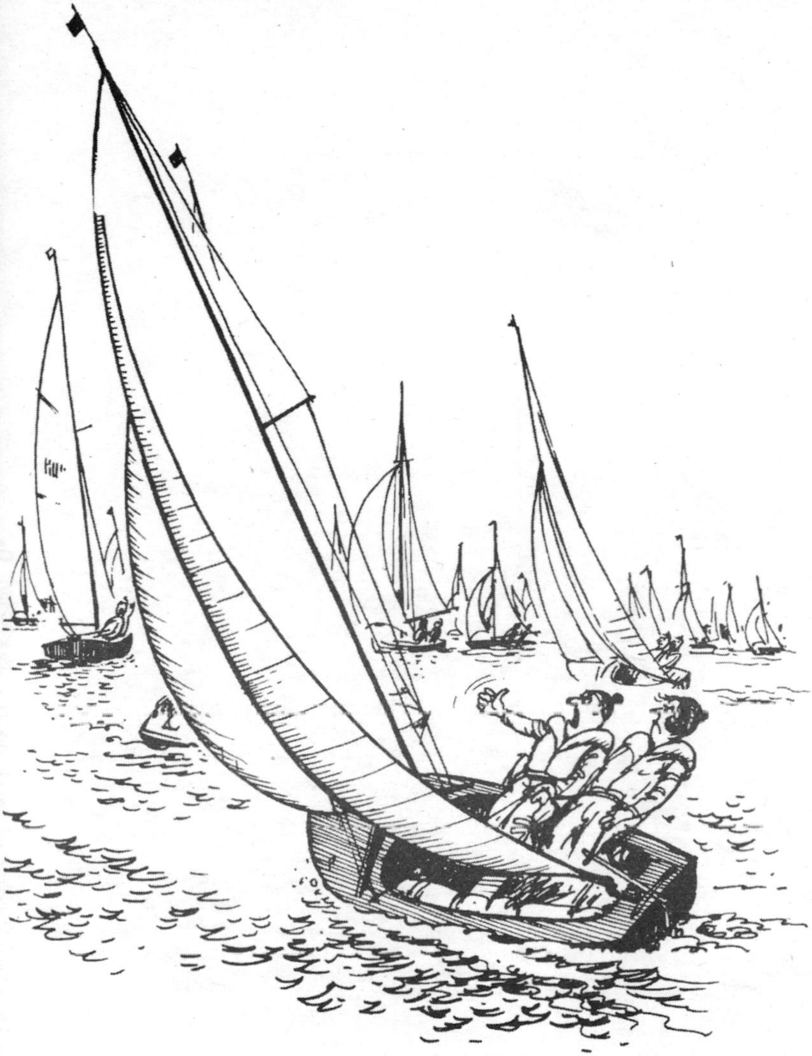

but one may spend many hours afloat without seeing
another human being.

The sea angler likes to dig his own bait
whenever possible

and to learn at first hand the intricacies of tides and currents.

He has his own peculiar problems whether casting
from the beach . . .

or from a boat.

For successful sea fishing the type of tackle must be
appropriate to the kind of fish one wishes to catch

and warm sensible clothing is vital for full enjoyment
of the sport.

A knowledge of where the fish are likely to be located
can save hours of frustration

and the ability to handle the catch is essential.

Full use should be made of sea objects put there
for your convenience.

The best places to fish may be learnt by watching
the experts

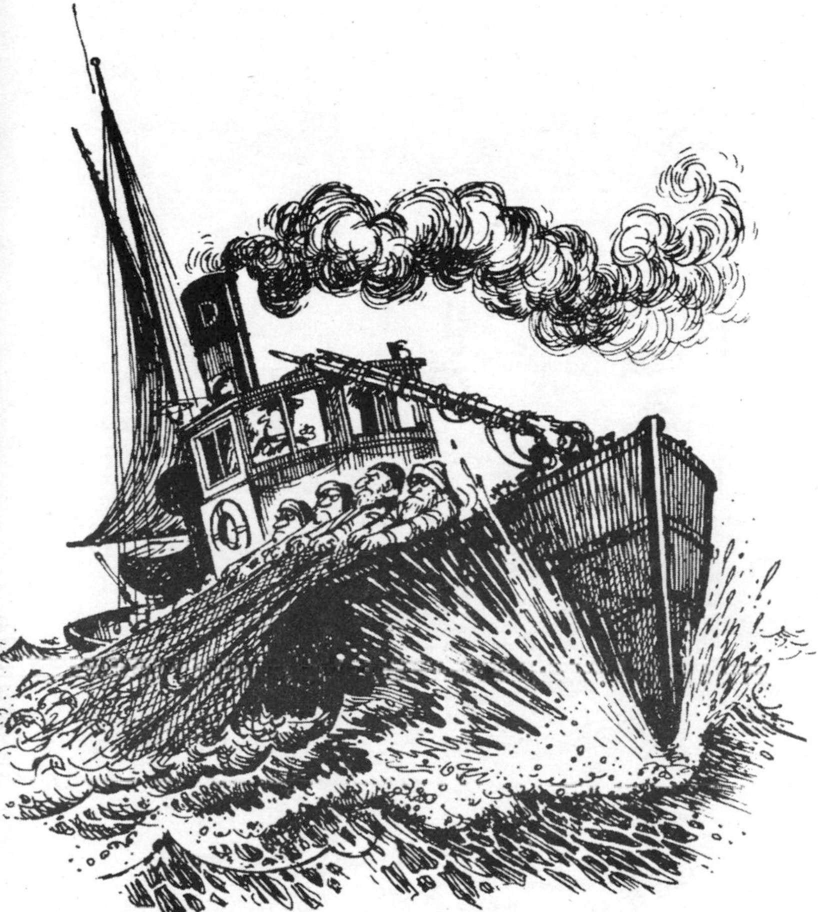

and by keeping an eye open for sea birds – they have an uncanny ability to locate fish.

When after a really big fish, the line must be strong
enough to avoid breakages

and it is advisable to understand the language
of the sea.

And above all . . .

Watch out for signs of bad weather – getting a boat
home in adverse conditions . . .

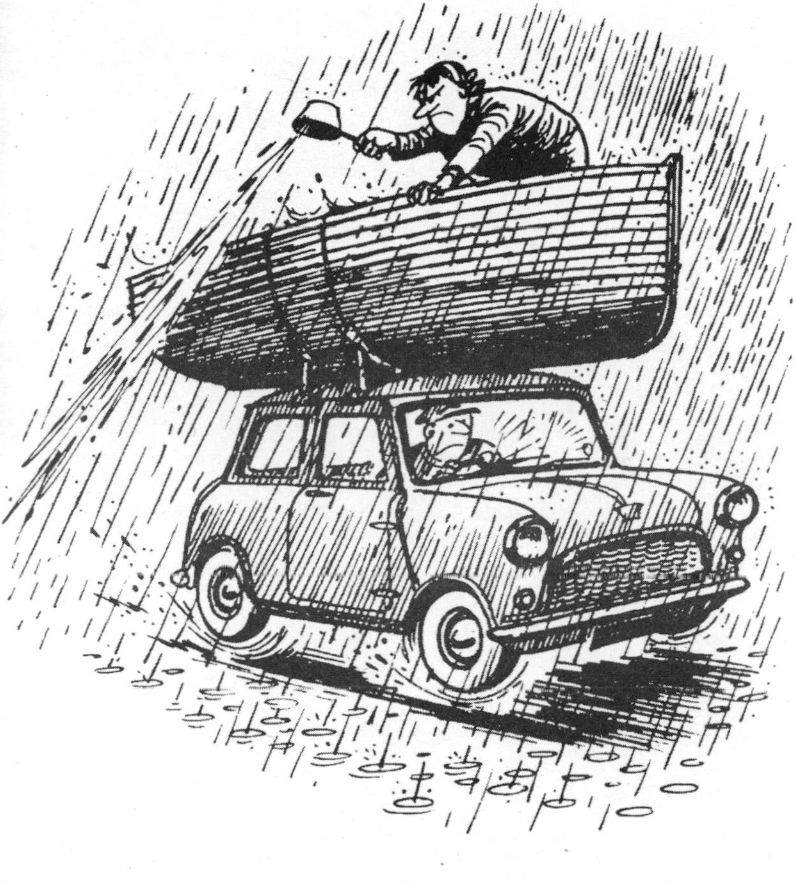

can prove very tricky.

ANGLER'S ETIQUETTE

Never begrudge spectators their interest in your
piscatorial prowess.

On no account trample growing crops . . .

or cause annoyance to farm animals.

Do not take fish by unauthorised means.

Be prepared to listen to the opinions of other anglers

and to give them the benefit of your own experience
in return.

It is unforgivable to impede a fellow angler . . .

who is trying to land a fish . . .

Or to leave litter about after a day's pleasure.
And finally . . .

if you think you have caught a record fish – make sure
you have a witness

and on no account dispose of it until all necessary facts
have been verified.

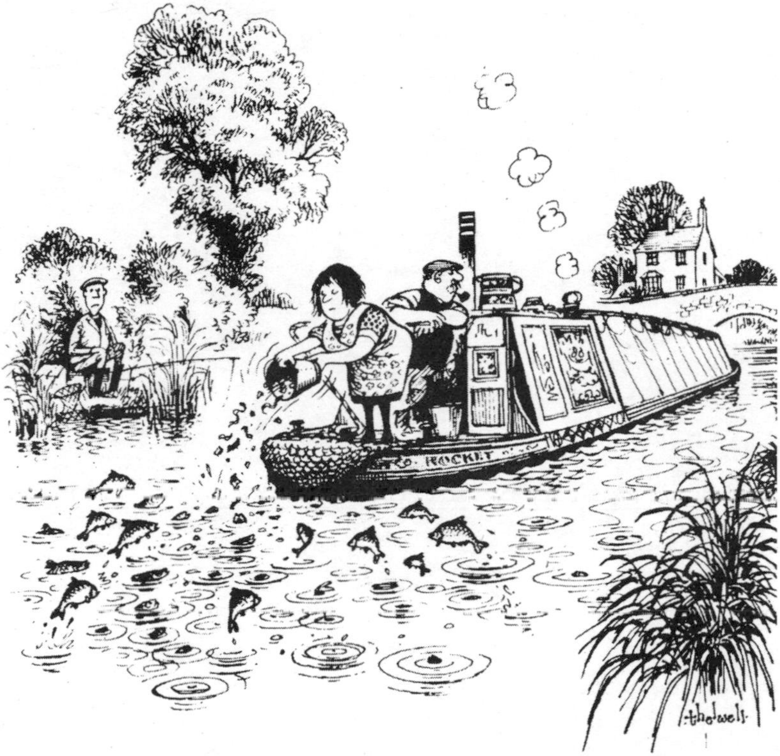
ROCKET

MORE FROM BRITAIN'S BEST LOVED CARTOONIST

BRITAIN'S BELOVED CARTOONIST

:thelwell.

UP THE GARDEN PATH

Instant grassification!

The perfect gift for any gardener who has experienced over-
bearing neighbours, the pains of building a water feature,
unruly indoor plants; and the battle to dig the lawnmower out
from the shed. Britain's beloved cartoonist Norman Thelwell
presents a fine crop of witticisms in his hilarious gardener's
handbook.

Garden fencing

Mites

BRITAIN'S BELOVED CARTOONIST

:thelwell.

PLAY IT
AS IT LIES

NORMAN THELWELL CENTENARY

A howl in one!

The perfect gift for any golfer who has experienced the horrors of sporting the wrong attire on course, losing his ball, or been wronged by unforgivable gamesmanship. Britain's beloved cartoonist Norman Thelwell scores a hole-in-one with his rollicking golfer's manual.

If you can swat a fly with a rolled-up newspaper . . .

or knock the head off a daisy with a stick – you can
play golf.

BRITAIN'S BELOVED CARTOONIST

thelwell.

THREE SHEETS IN THE WIND

NORMAN THELWELL CENTENARY

A luff a minute!

The perfect gift for any sailor who has misinterpreted a distress signal, worn stilettos on board, abandoned ship, or experienced irreparable damage to their social status at the club. Britain's beloved cartoonist Norman Thelwell will have you in fits of luffter with his indispensable manual of instruction for sailors everywhere.

A sea shanty

Free board

NORMAN THELWELL contributed more than 1,600 cartoons to Punch magazine, the *Sunday Express* and Tatler. Thelwell's cartoons remain a popular and wry look at British life. He was particularly well-known for his cartoons on horse riding, fishing, sailing, motoring and country pursuits and was one of the founder members of the British Cartoonists' Association.

thelwell.org.uk